AF413250

My Love Letter to Alcohol

Recovery from a Drowned Relationship

Christina L Cloud

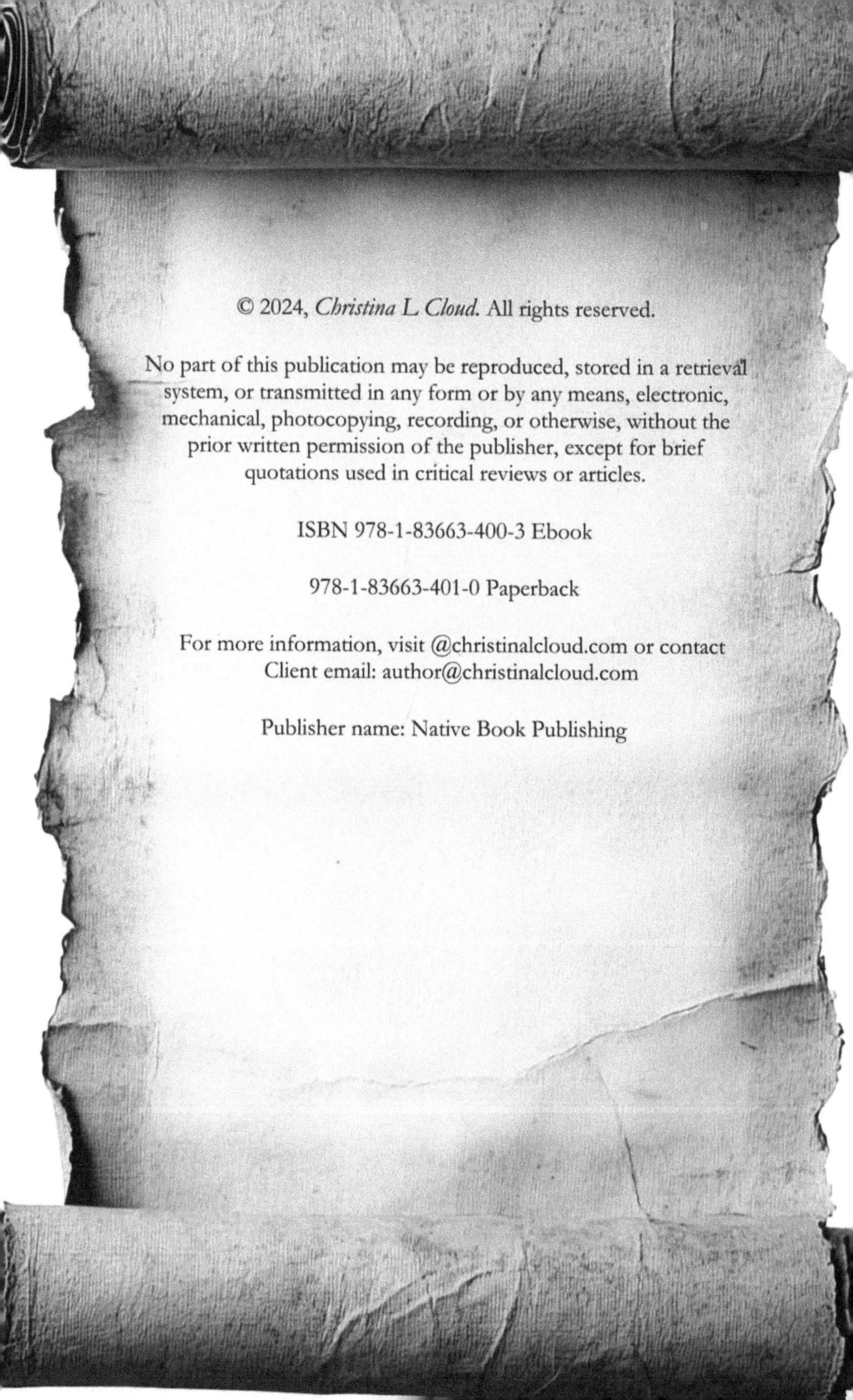

ISBN 978-1-83663-400-3 Ebook

978-1-83663-401-0 Paperback

For more information, visit @christinalcloud.com or contact Client email: author@christinalcloud.com

Publisher name: Native Book Publishing

Table of Contents

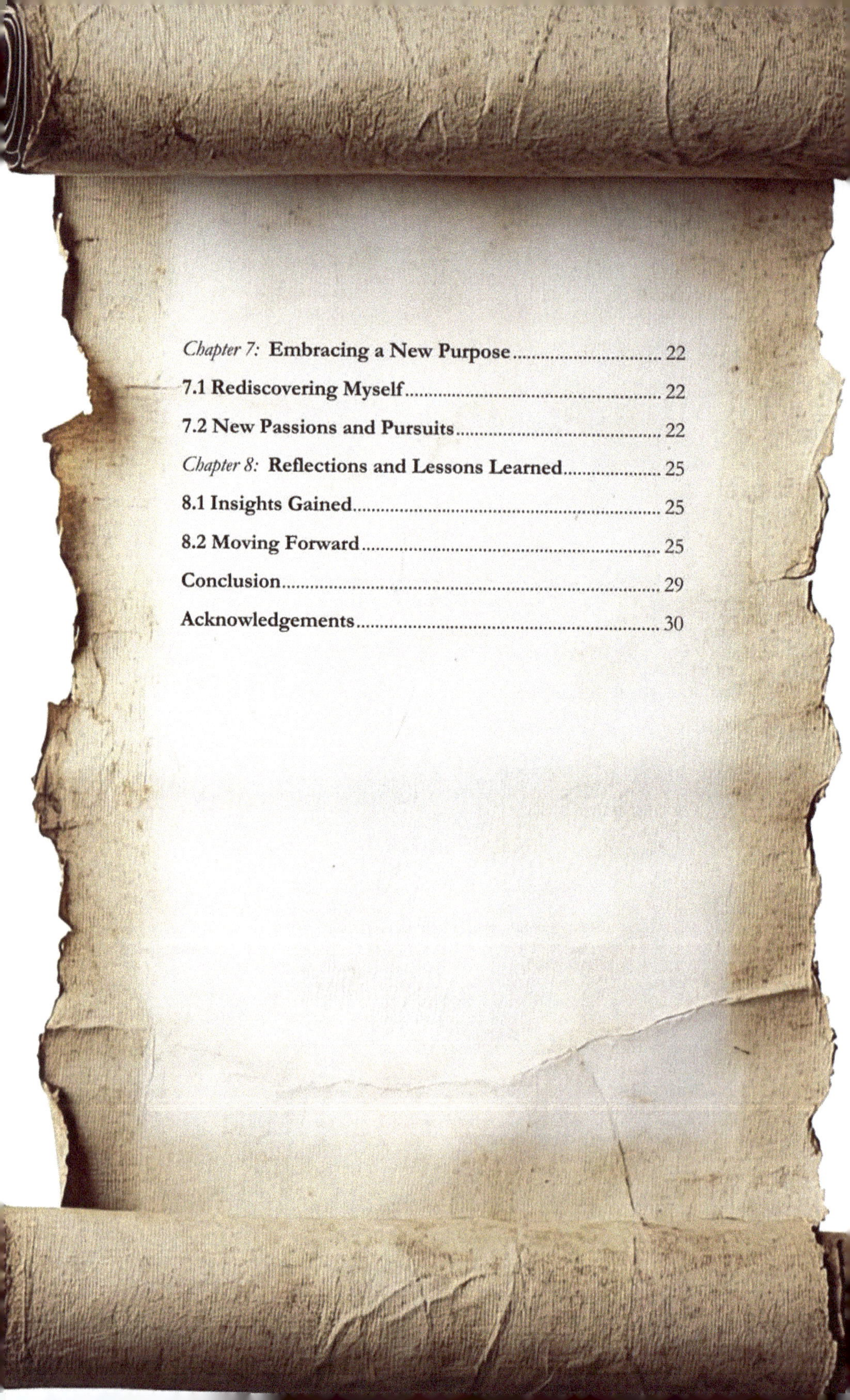

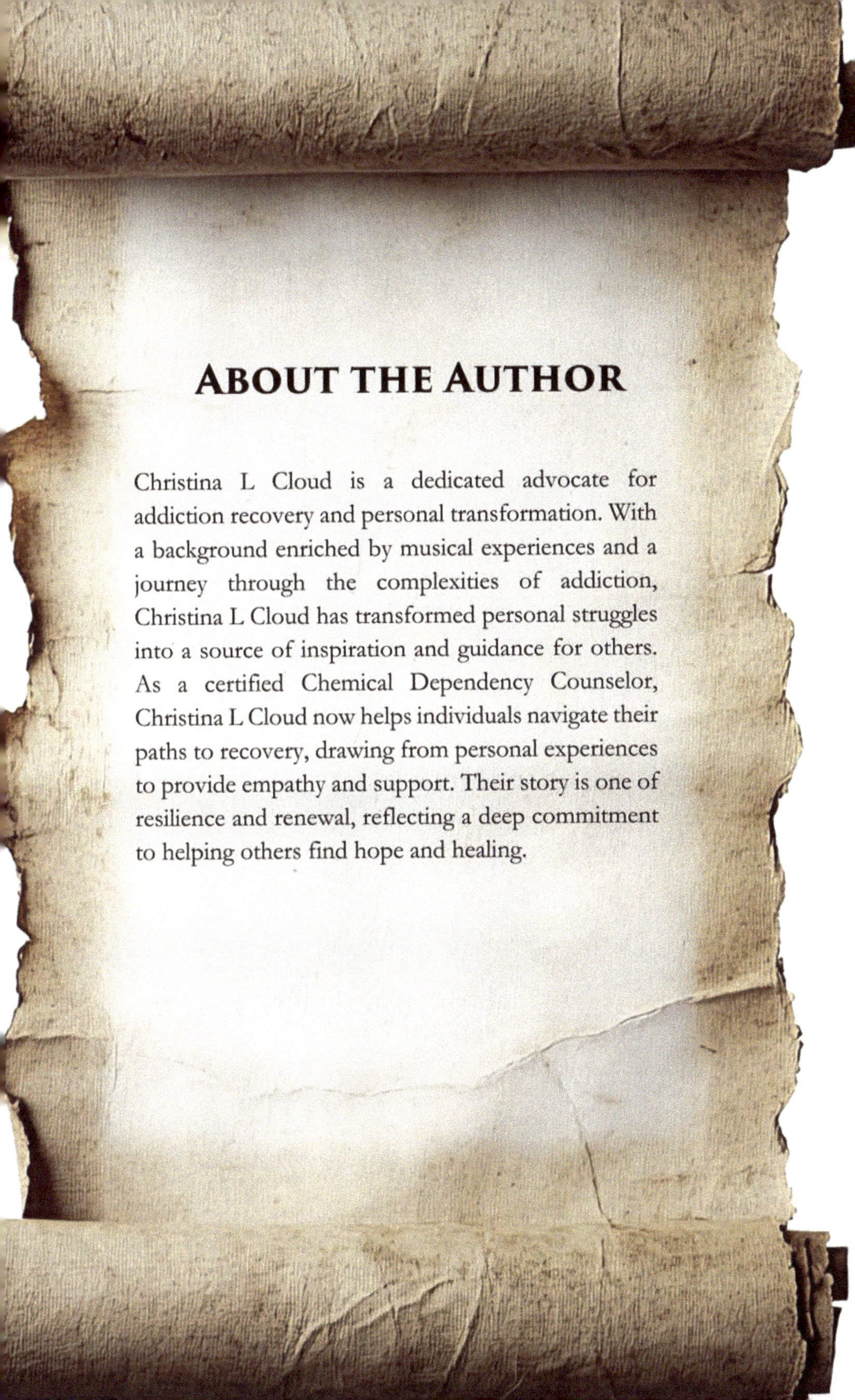

ABOUT THE AUTHOR

Christina L Cloud is a dedicated advocate for addiction recovery and personal transformation. With a background enriched by musical experiences and a journey through the complexities of addiction, Christina L Cloud has transformed personal struggles into a source of inspiration and guidance for others. As a certified Chemical Dependency Counselor, Christina L Cloud now helps individuals navigate their paths to recovery, drawing from personal experiences to provide empathy and support. Their story is one of resilience and renewal, reflecting a deep commitment to helping others find hope and healing.

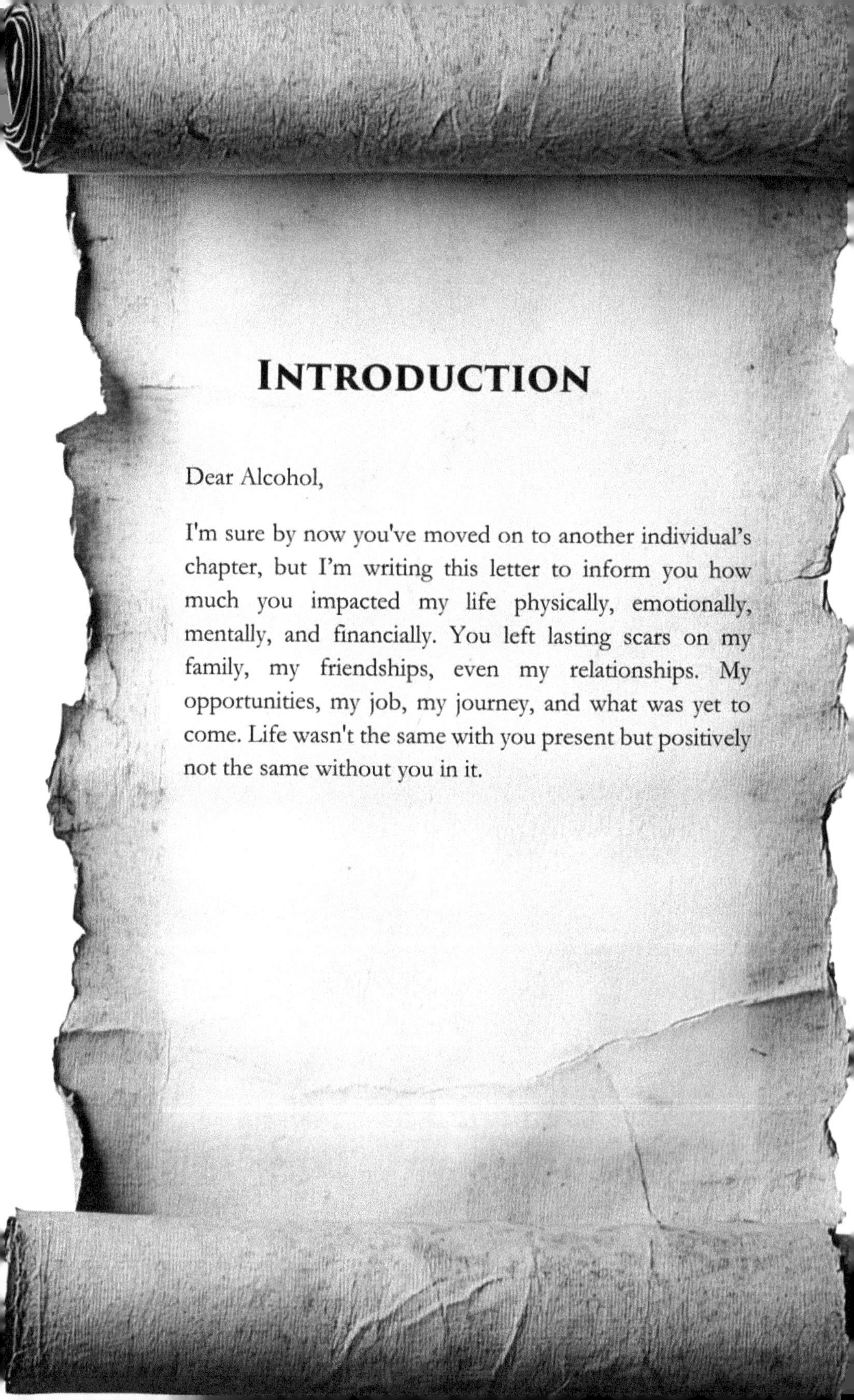

INTRODUCTION

Dear Alcohol,

I'm sure by now you've moved on to another individual's chapter, but I'm writing this letter to inform you how much you impacted my life physically, emotionally, mentally, and financially. You left lasting scars on my family, my friendships, even my relationships. My opportunities, my job, my journey, and what was yet to come. Life wasn't the same with you present but positively not the same without you in it.

MY FIRST ENCOUNTER

1.1 THE EARLY DAYS

When I first came into contact with you, it felt like an invitation from the universe, orchestrated by mutual friends who didn't know what they were unleashing. If I had a type, you were it—charismatic, enticing, and full of promise. At that time, I was just a single young woman living on my own, navigating life with a predictable routine of work, church, and the occasional gig playing drums. My life was simple, yet there were questions lingering in my mind, unanswered and echoing in the quiet moments.

Growing up with a single mother, I saw her struggle to provide the best life she could for me. She was my rock, yet I often sensed a void. Our home life was structured and straightforward, a comforting cocoon of support, but there was still something missing—a father's presence. My biological father was largely absent, entangled in his own battles, leaving me with feelings of rejection and unanswered questions.

When I was eight, everything shifted. My mother married a kind and hardworking man who took me under his wing. One day, he sat me down and told me he had legally adopted me and changed my last name. I was cautious; no man had ever taken on that responsibility for me. Yet, as he spoke, I felt a weight lift off my shoulders. For the first time, I experienced the warmth of a father's love, even if it was fleeting. He would be in my life for only a short time, but the memories we created together became treasures I hold close to my heart.

Those early days shaped my longing for connection and belonging, a yearning that you seemed to fulfill. I welcomed you into my life, unaware of the tumultuous journey we would embark on together. What started as a fleeting escape quickly spiraled into something far more complex. But in those initial moments, I was simply looking for joy, connection, and a way to fill the void that had lingered for so long

1.2 THE FIRST SIP

At that party, surrounded by laughter and anticipation, I took my first sip of champagne. The sharpness burned my throat, but within moments, warmth spread through me. I felt invincible, carefree, and for the first time in a long while, I believed I belonged.

But that exhilaration was fleeting. I stumbled home that night, unsure of how I had made it back. I promised myself I would never let it get that out of control again. Yet, as time went on, I found myself drawn back into the haze, curious about what I had tasted.

Chapter 1 – My First Encounter

How did Christina's early experiences with family and identity shape her initial attraction to alcohol? In what ways can early emotional voids influence future dependencies?

____

____

____

____

____

____

____

____

____

____

CHAPTER 2

THE ALLURE OF ALCOHOL

2.1 BOOSTING CONFIDENCE

You quickly became my source of confidence. In social situations, I could shed my shyness and engage freely. Conversations became effortless, and I danced like no one was watching. The insecurities that had plagued me melted away.

But deep down, I knew this confidence was a facade. My interactions with others were often driven by the drinks, not by genuine connection. I wondered if people would still accept me if they saw me without that liquid courage. I became a performer in a world fueled by alcohol..

2.2 SOCIAL DYNAMICS

Alcohol became a constant companion in my social life. I planned my activities around drinking, creating a delicate dance between work, obligations, and my need

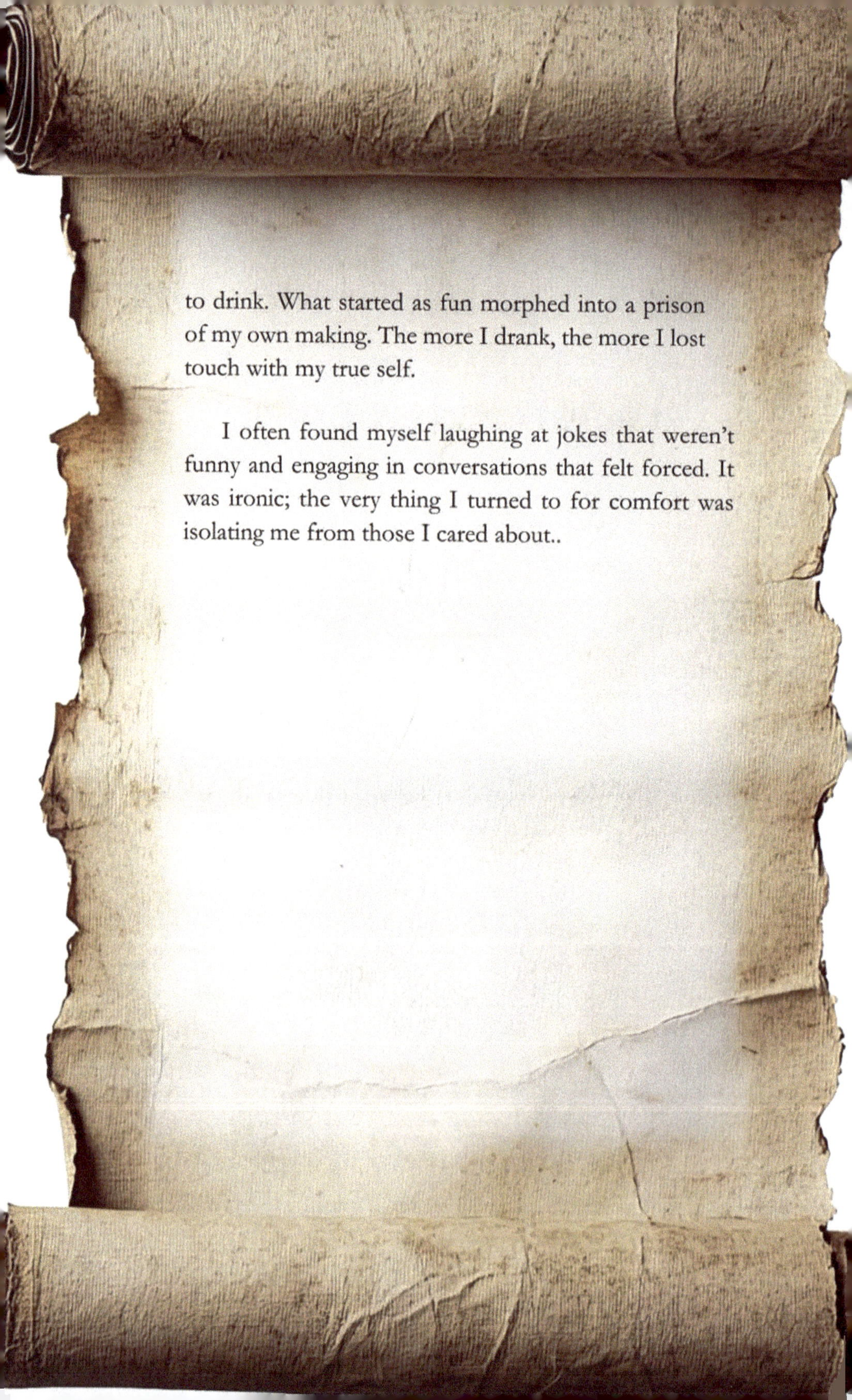

to drink. What started as fun morphed into a prison of my own making. The more I drank, the more I lost touch with my true self.

I often found myself laughing at jokes that weren't funny and engaging in conversations that felt forced. It was ironic; the very thing I turned to for comfort was isolating me from those I cared about..

What does the author reveal about the illusion of confidence alcohol provides? How can we distinguish between authentic self-expression and substance-fueled personas

____

____

____

____

____

____

____

____

____

____

____

CHAPTER 3:

THE DEPENDENCY GROWS

3.1 DAILY RITUALS

As alcohol became part of my daily routine, I found myself trapped in a cycle. Mornings began with headaches, and I learned to relieve the pain with another drink. Each day felt like a battle between my desire to drink and my hope for a better life.

Promises of "just one drink" quickly turned into spirals of excess. I realized I was no longer in control; I was being pulled deeper into the depths of my addiction. I felt like a prisoner, chained to my dependence.

3.2 PHYSICAL AND EMOTIONAL IMPACT

The toll of my drinking became evident. I struggled with persistent hangovers, weight fluctuations, and health issues. I battled insomnia, waking up in the middle of the night with racing thoughts. I looked in the mirror and saw a stranger— a shadow of the person I once was.

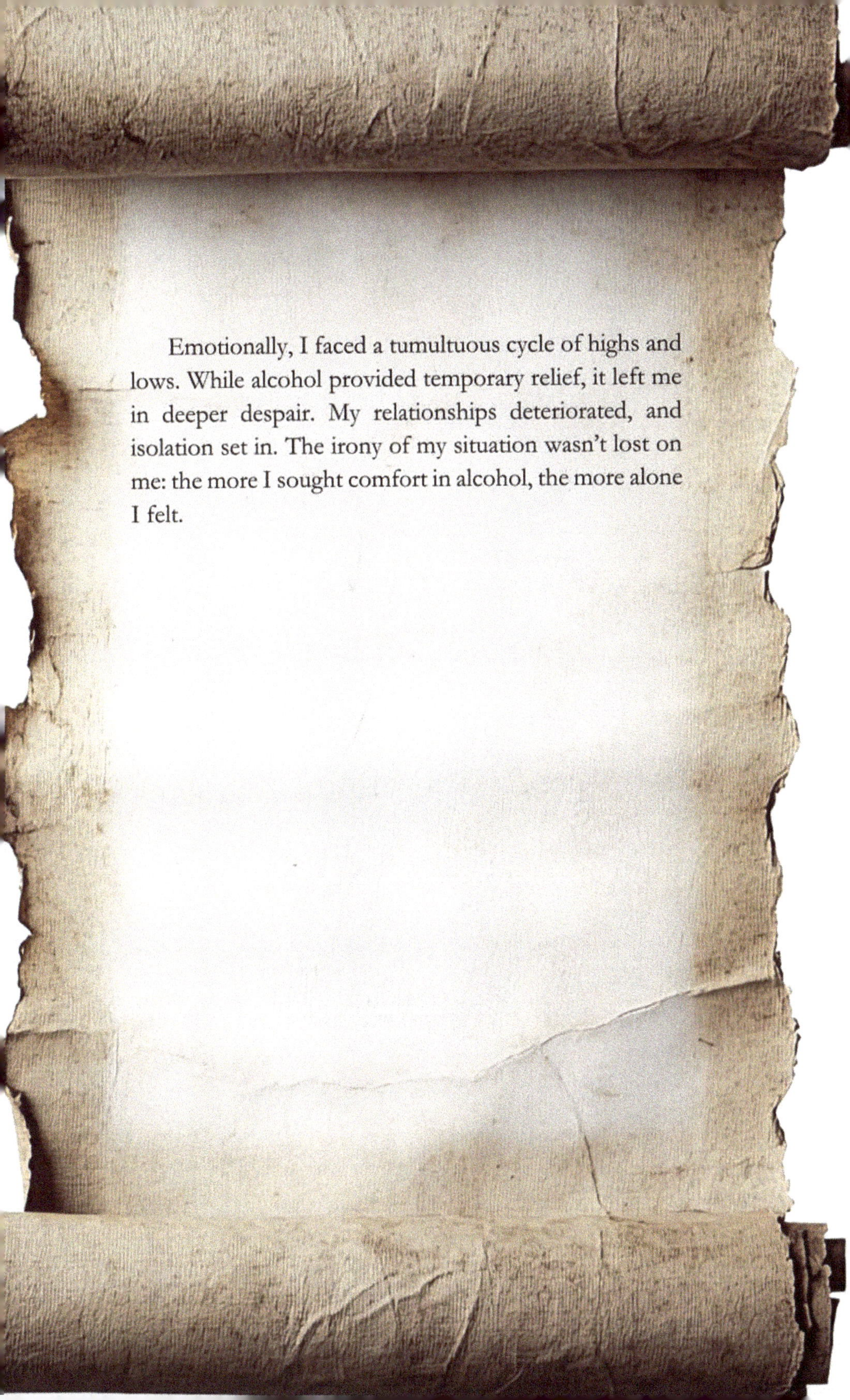

Emotionally, I faced a tumultuous cycle of highs and lows. While alcohol provided temporary relief, it left me in deeper despair. My relationships deteriorated, and isolation set in. The irony of my situation wasn't lost on me: the more I sought comfort in alcohol, the more alone I felt.

Chapter 3 – The Dependency Grows

What signs of addiction does Christina describe that may often go unnoticed in everyday life? How can we become more aware of these subtle shifts in ourselves or others?

CHAPTER 4:
STRUGGLES TO BREAK FREE

4.1 ATTEMPTS AT RECOVERY

I sought various methods to break free, from AA meetings to therapy. I sat in those circles, listening to others share their stories, feeling a mix of hope and shame. Each time I left, I questioned if I would ever be able to share my own story without feeling like an imposter.

Despite my efforts, each attempt felt inadequate. I often felt like I was chasing a mirage, where each moment of clarity faded into a fog of despair. The pressure to recover weighed heavily on me, and each failure felt like a mark against my worth.

4.2 FACING THE TRUTH

Confronting the reality of my addiction was painful. I had to look at my fears and weaknesses head-on. I began journaling my thoughts, pouring my heart onto the pages. Writing became a therapeutic outlet, a way to process my emotions and untangle the mess inside me.

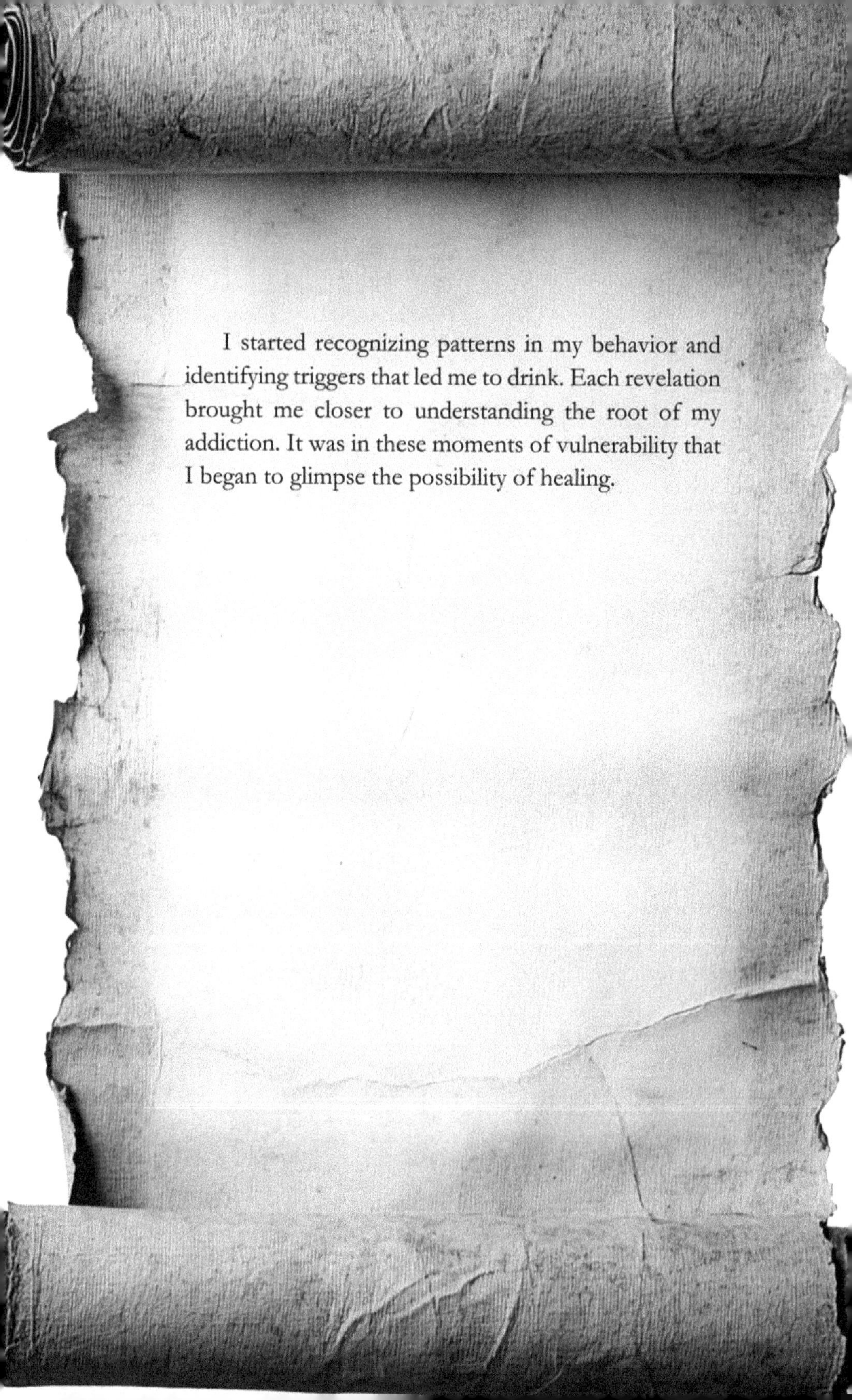

I started recognizing patterns in my behavior and identifying triggers that led me to drink. Each revelation brought me closer to understanding the root of my addiction. It was in these moments of vulnerability that I began to glimpse the possibility of healing.

Chapter 4 – Struggles to Break Free

What internal and external barriers did Christina face in her attempts to recover? How do shame and self-doubt complicate the recovery process?

____

____

____

____

____

____

____

____

____

____

____

CHAPTER 5:
MOMENTS OF CLARITY

5.1 THE HOSPITAL EXPERIENCE

One pivotal moment came during a hospital stay. I lay in that sterile room, facing the consequences of my choices. I listened to the beeping machines and saw the worry on my loved ones' faces. It hit me hard: I had to choose between continuing down this destructive path or fighting for my life.

In that vulnerable space, I realized I had the power to change my narrative. I saw the impact of my addiction on my family and friends, and I knew I had to do better.

5.2 KEY CONVERSATIONS

During my hospital stay, I had profound conversations with doctors, nurses, and fellow patients. One nurse, in particular, shared her own recovery story, igniting a spark of hope within me. Her journey resonated deeply, showing me that change was possible.

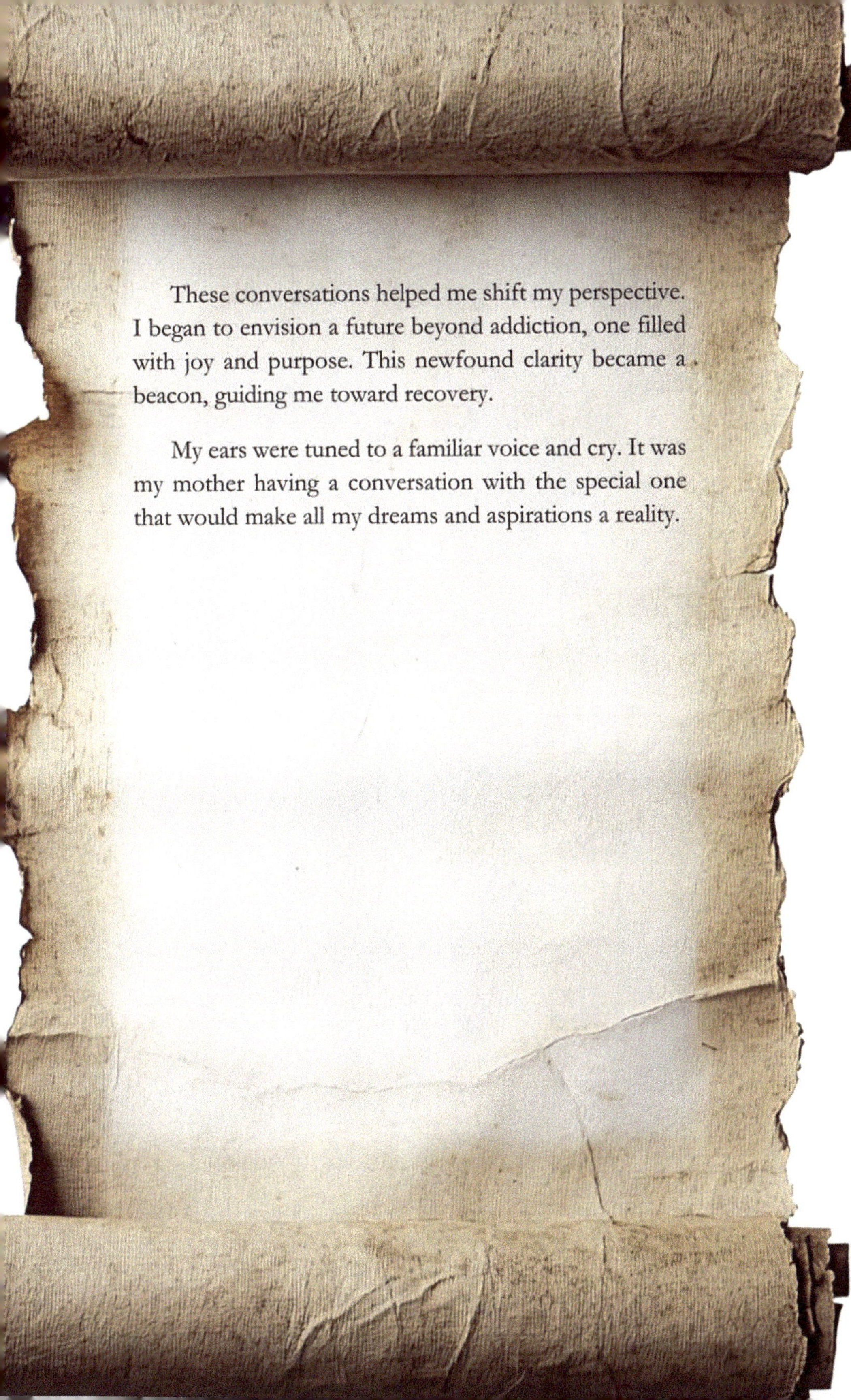

These conversations helped me shift my perspective. I began to envision a future beyond addiction, one filled with joy and purpose. This newfound clarity became a beacon, guiding me toward recovery.

My ears were tuned to a familiar voice and cry. It was my mother having a conversation with the special one that would make all my dreams and aspirations a reality.

Chapter 5 – Moments of Clarity

How did the hospital experience and conversations with others serve as a turning point for Christina? What role does empathy from others play in personal transformation?

CHAPTER 6:
THE TURNING POINT

6.1 SUPPORT FROM AN UNEXPECTED SOURCE

A turning point in my journey came from an unexpected source. This person believed in me, offering support and encouragement when I needed it most. Their genuine concern made me see a future beyond my addiction. I remember sitting with them, feeling the weight of their faith in me, and for the first time, I began to believe in myself.

This connection taught me that vulnerability can be a strength. I learned that asking for help was not a sign of weakness but a vital step in my healing journey.

6.2 EMBRACING A NEW PERSPECTIVE

Embracing a new perspective marked the beginning of real change. I started setting achievable goals focused

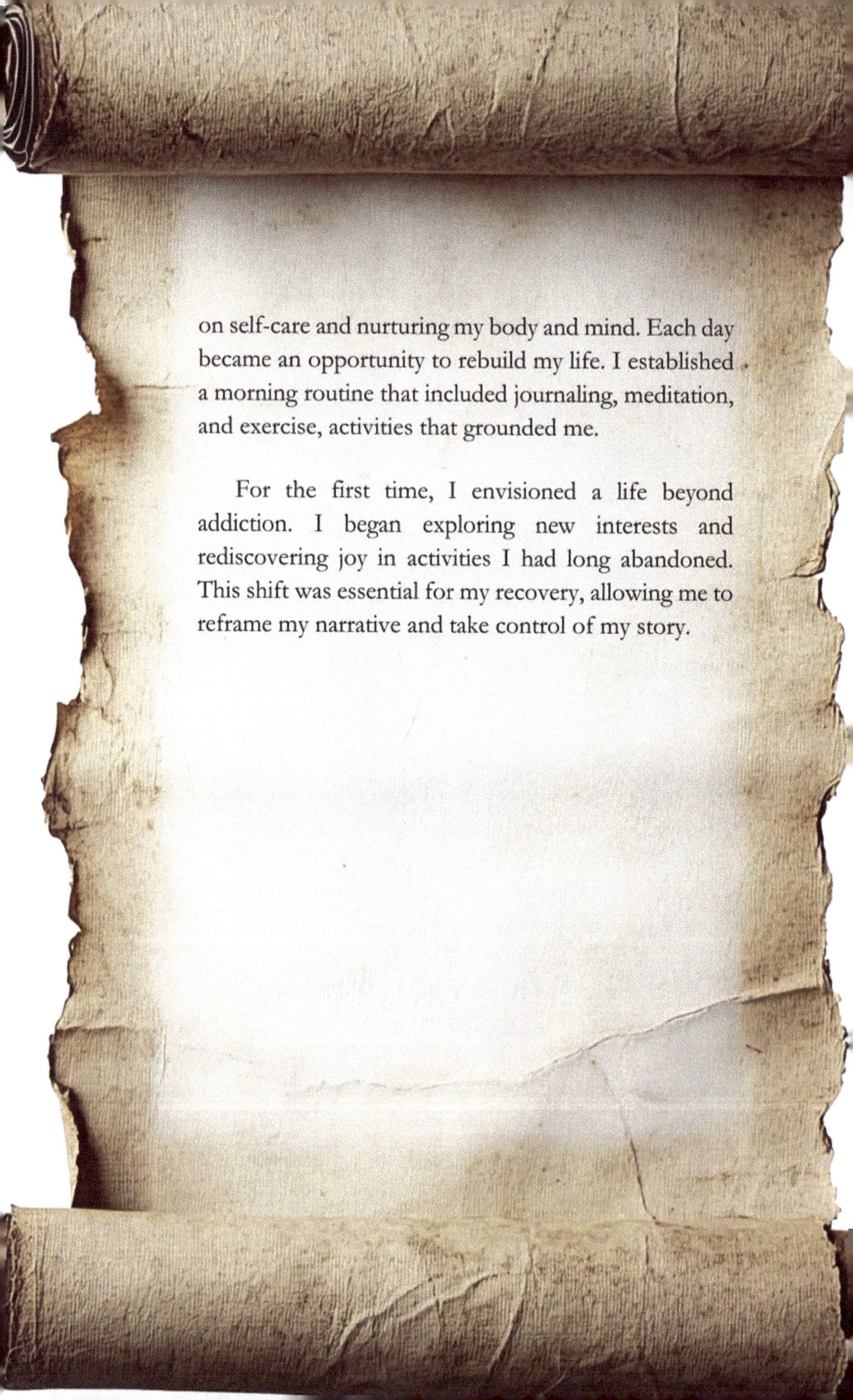

on self-care and nurturing my body and mind. Each day became an opportunity to rebuild my life. I established a morning routine that included journaling, meditation, and exercise, activities that grounded me.

For the first time, I envisioned a life beyond addiction. I began exploring new interests and rediscovering joy in activities I had long abandoned. This shift was essential for my recovery, allowing me to reframe my narrative and take control of my story.

Chapter 6 – The Turning Point

What impact did support from an unexpected source have on Christina's journey? How can one person's belief in us change the trajectory of our lives?

____

____

____

____

____

____

____

____

____

____

____

____

____

____

CHAPTER 7

EMBRACING A NEW PURPOSE

7.1 REDISCOVERING MYSELF

In recovery, I began to rediscover my true self. My relationships improved as I learned to communicate openly and honestly. I found joy in new passions, such as becoming a certified Chemical Dependency Counselor, channeling my experiences to support others. I realized that my struggles could empower others on their own journeys.

I immersed myself in workshops, connecting with like-minded individuals who shared my passion for recovery. Through this work, I found a sense of belonging that I had long sought.

7.2 NEW PASSIONS AND PURSUITS

With renewed purpose, I explored new interests like volunteering and public speaking. Sharing my story at local events became a source of fulfillment, helping me create connections with others who shared my passion for recovery.

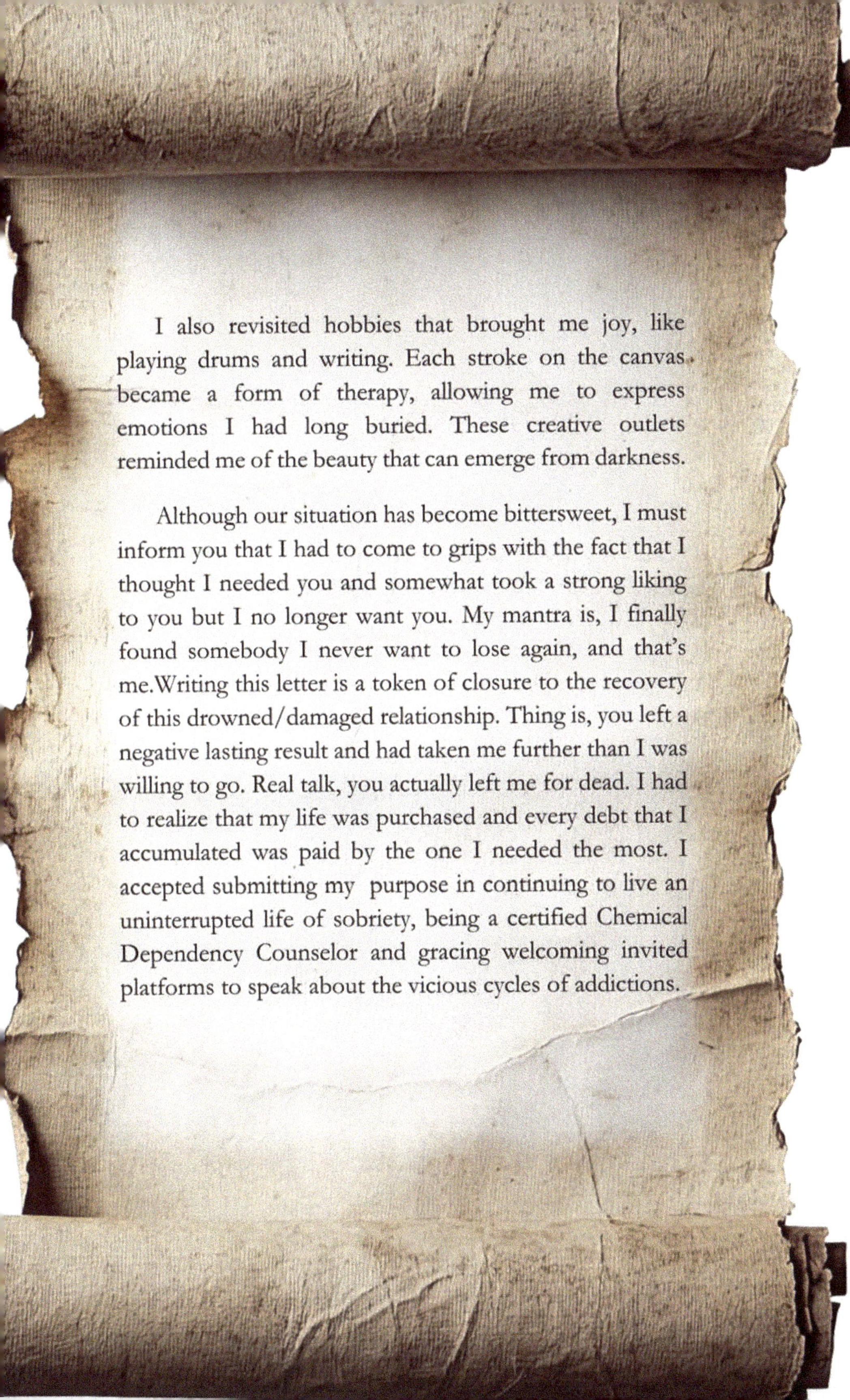

I also revisited hobbies that brought me joy, like playing drums and writing. Each stroke on the canvas became a form of therapy, allowing me to express emotions I had long buried. These creative outlets reminded me of the beauty that can emerge from darkness.

Although our situation has become bittersweet, I must inform you that I had to come to grips with the fact that I thought I needed you and somewhat took a strong liking to you but I no longer want you. My mantra is, I finally found somebody I never want to lose again, and that's me.Writing this letter is a token of closure to the recovery of this drowned/damaged relationship. Thing is, you left a negative lasting result and had taken me further than I was willing to go. Real talk, you actually left me for dead. I had to realize that my life was purchased and every debt that I accumulated was paid by the one I needed the most. I accepted submitting my purpose in continuing to live an uninterrupted life of sobriety, being a certified Chemical Dependency Counselor and gracing welcoming invited platforms to speak about the vicious cycles of addictions.

Chapter 7 – Embracing a New Purpose

How did Christina's sense of identity evolve as she embraced recovery? What does her story teach us about finding purpose through pain?

CHAPTER 8:
REFLECTIONS & LESSONS LEARNED

8.1 INSIGHTS GAINED

Reflecting on my journey, I've gained profound insights into addiction and recovery. I learned that recovery is not linear; it's a journey filled with setbacks and triumphs. Each experience taught me about resilience and the importance of community support.

I came to understand that vulnerability fosters connection and healing. Self-compassion became crucial; I learned to forgive myself for past mistakes, recognizing that they were part of my journey, not my identity.

8.2 MOVING FORWARD

Moving forward, I remain committed to maintaining my sobriety and helping others. My experiences shape my approach to life, fueling my desire to live a purposeful and fulfilling life. I am no longer defined by my addiction; I embrace each day as an opportunity for growth and gratitude.

As I navigate life, I hold onto the lessons learned and the relationships forged along the way. Recovery is an ongoing journey, requiring continual effort and reflection. Each day presents a chance to be better, to learn more, and to impact the lives of others positively..

This experience was not just for me but for others to know not to misuse you either. I have allowed my failures to teach me and not torment me. I decided to conquer my failures and not let my failures conquer me. I made up my mind not to just exist but live. My purpose and assignment is not to be a radar for others' downfall regarding you but my life is now about affirmation, renewal and reflection. With this I can be a light, listening ear and safe resource to help aid and guide others through personal mishaps. I guess you can say I went through a makeover process. In all honesty I really experienced a mental, physical and spiritual rebirth. My greatest accomplishment was learning to love myself. So today I stand being put back together again after being broken. Even off of broken pieces, I made it. All in a nutshell because of you, my public humiliation has become my historical success. The miraculous thing is, it was shared with my family that I would die while being unresponsive for months. As I overcame that, it was said that I would never be the same person mentally ever again. It was also told to me that I would have to have two transplants and the list goes on. I started wondering if any good thing come out of this. But God didn't see fit to let none of these things be. Actually, he has taken the sting out of my entire situation. Long story short, I SURVIVED, because there's more. This is my recovery in whom I am well pleased.

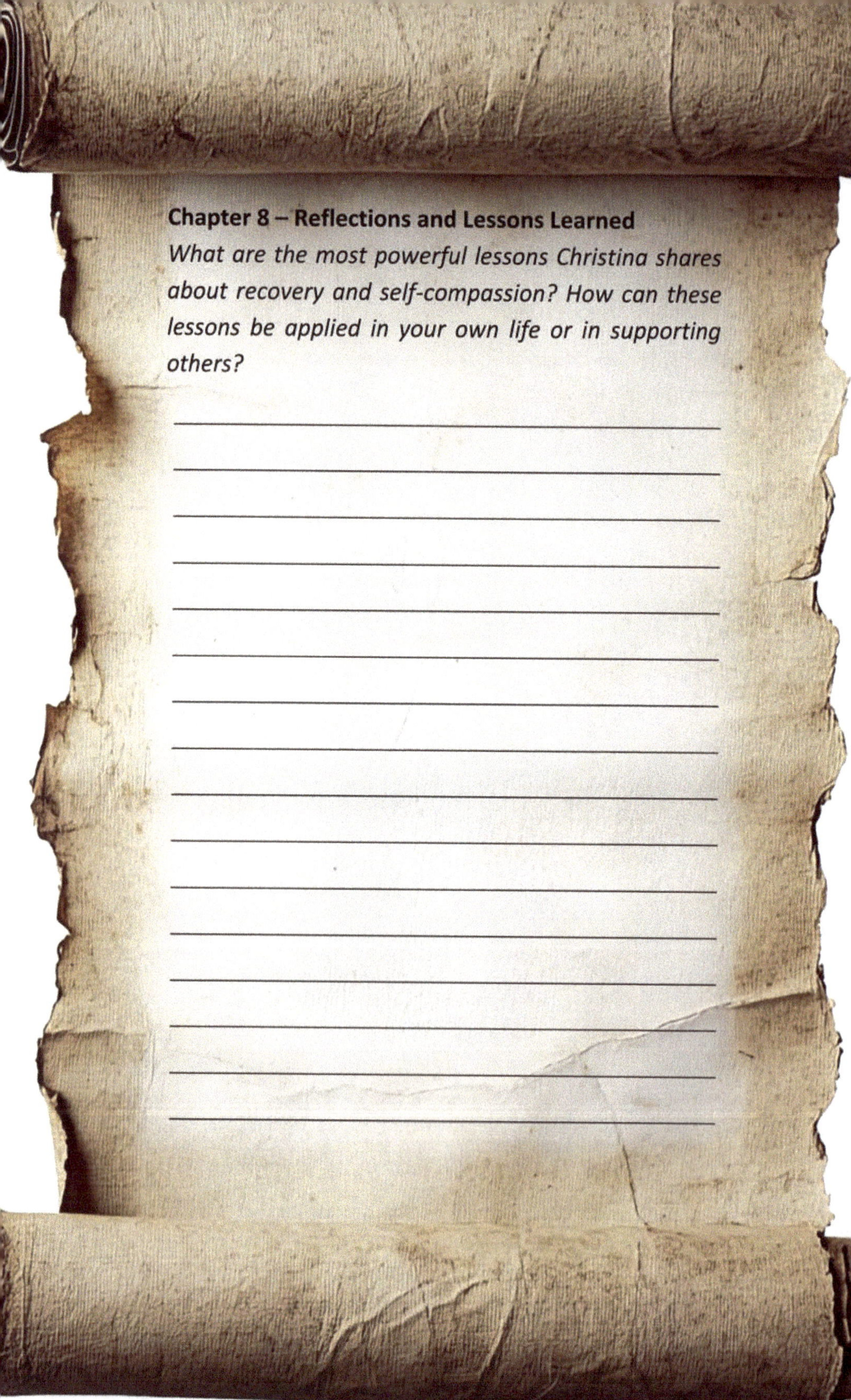

Chapter 8 – Reflections and Lessons Learned

What are the most powerful lessons Christina shares about recovery and self-compassion? How can these lessons be applied in your own life or in supporting others?

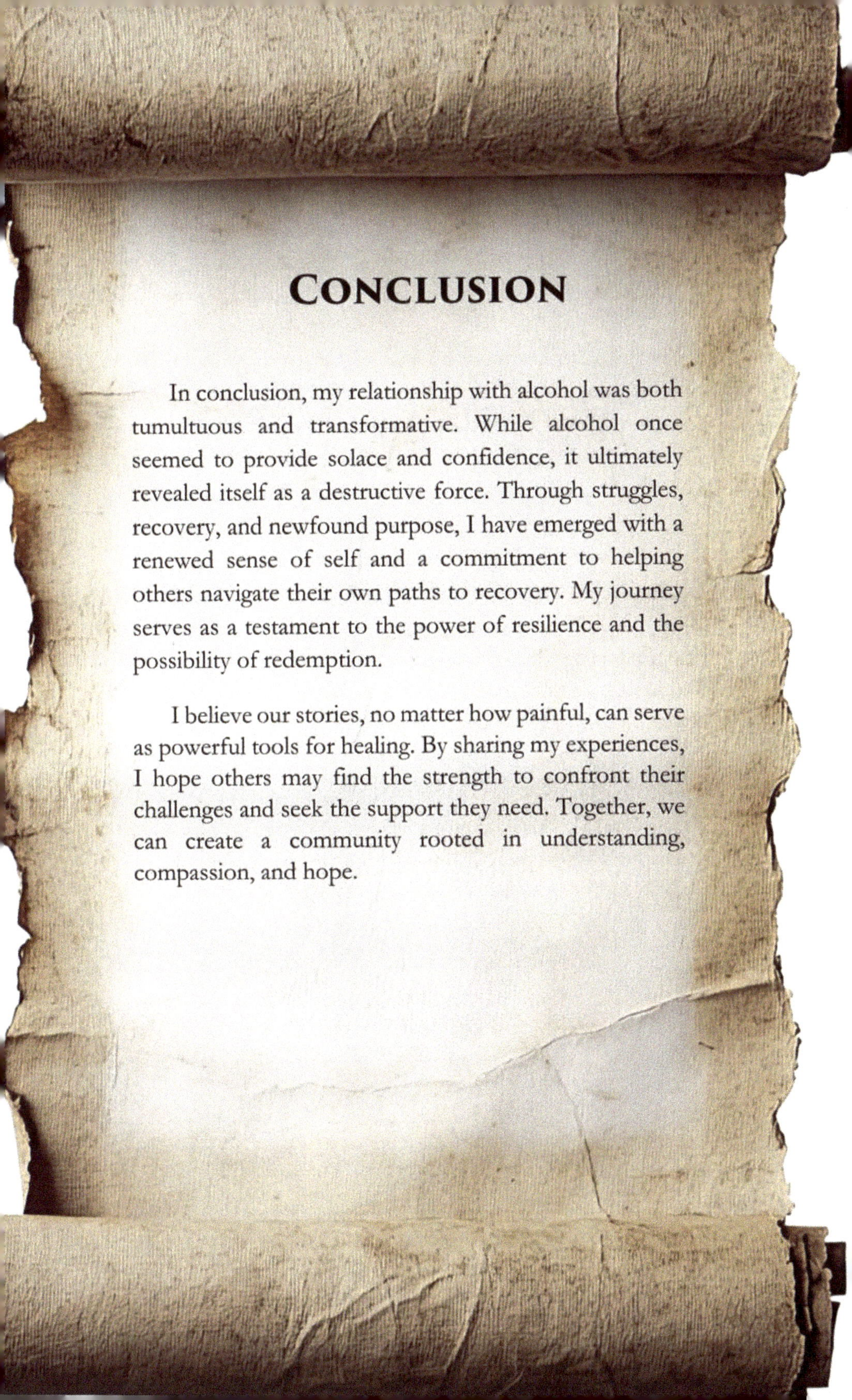

CONCLUSION

In conclusion, my relationship with alcohol was both tumultuous and transformative. While alcohol once seemed to provide solace and confidence, it ultimately revealed itself as a destructive force. Through struggles, recovery, and newfound purpose, I have emerged with a renewed sense of self and a commitment to helping others navigate their own paths to recovery. My journey serves as a testament to the power of resilience and the possibility of redemption.

I believe our stories, no matter how painful, can serve as powerful tools for healing. By sharing my experiences, I hope others may find the strength to confront their challenges and seek the support they need. Together, we can create a community rooted in understanding, compassion, and hope.

ACKNOWLEDGEMENTS

Special thanks to God for the miraculous handy work over my life. I'm grateful that you allowed your amazing restorative redeeming power to manifest after a hard journey. You saw the best in me and I'm forever thankful. To my mother, Legenda Cloud for exemplifying amazing strength, courage and support during my journey. You being there every step of the way made everything possible. Your love for me protected and covered me through what seemed to be the most painful experience of my life. We are strong because we made it through some tough, difficult and challenging times together. I could not have done it without you. You showed me how to endure hardness as a good soldier. Also, to my sister Ashley and her family for their unlimited support, prayers, encouragement and sacrifices. I'm alive because you followed your heart, mind and spirit. You are the best sister anyone could ever ask for. To my awesome friends, family and love ones who never gave up on me. I'm so much better now because of the supportive environment and energy you guys created for me. Also, to the entire Cleveland Clinic Medical team for expertise, professionalism and dedication to the work, gifts and care that you consistently provided during my time at every facility.

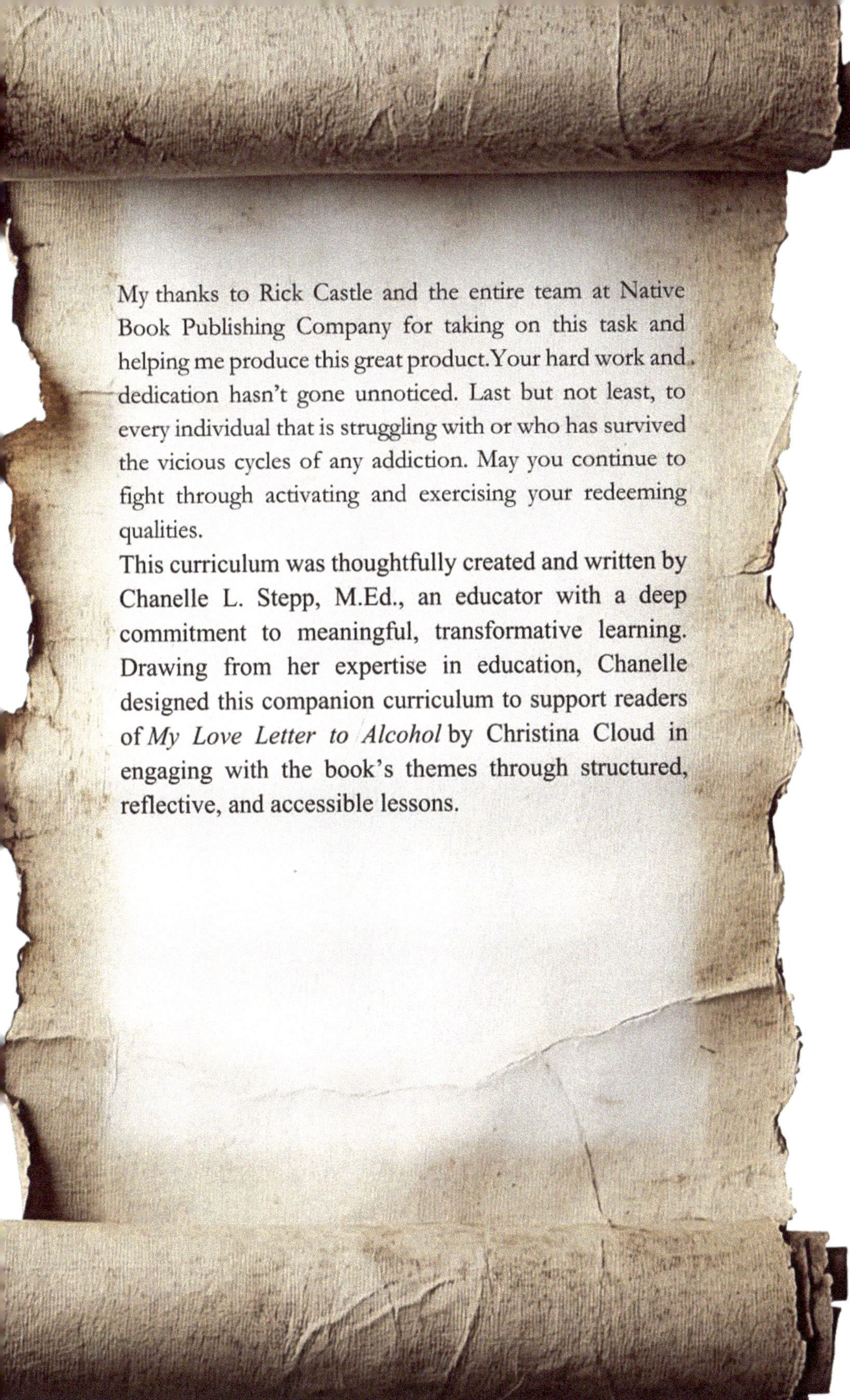

My thanks to Rick Castle and the entire team at Native Book Publishing Company for taking on this task and helping me produce this great product. Your hard work and dedication hasn't gone unnoticed. Last but not least, to every individual that is struggling with or who has survived the vicious cycles of any addiction. May you continue to fight through activating and exercising your redeeming qualities.

This curriculum was thoughtfully created and written by Chanelle L. Stepp, M.Ed., an educator with a deep commitment to meaningful, transformative learning. Drawing from her expertise in education, Chanelle designed this companion curriculum to support readers of *My Love Letter to Alcohol* by Christina Cloud in engaging with the book's themes through structured, reflective, and accessible lessons.

My Letter

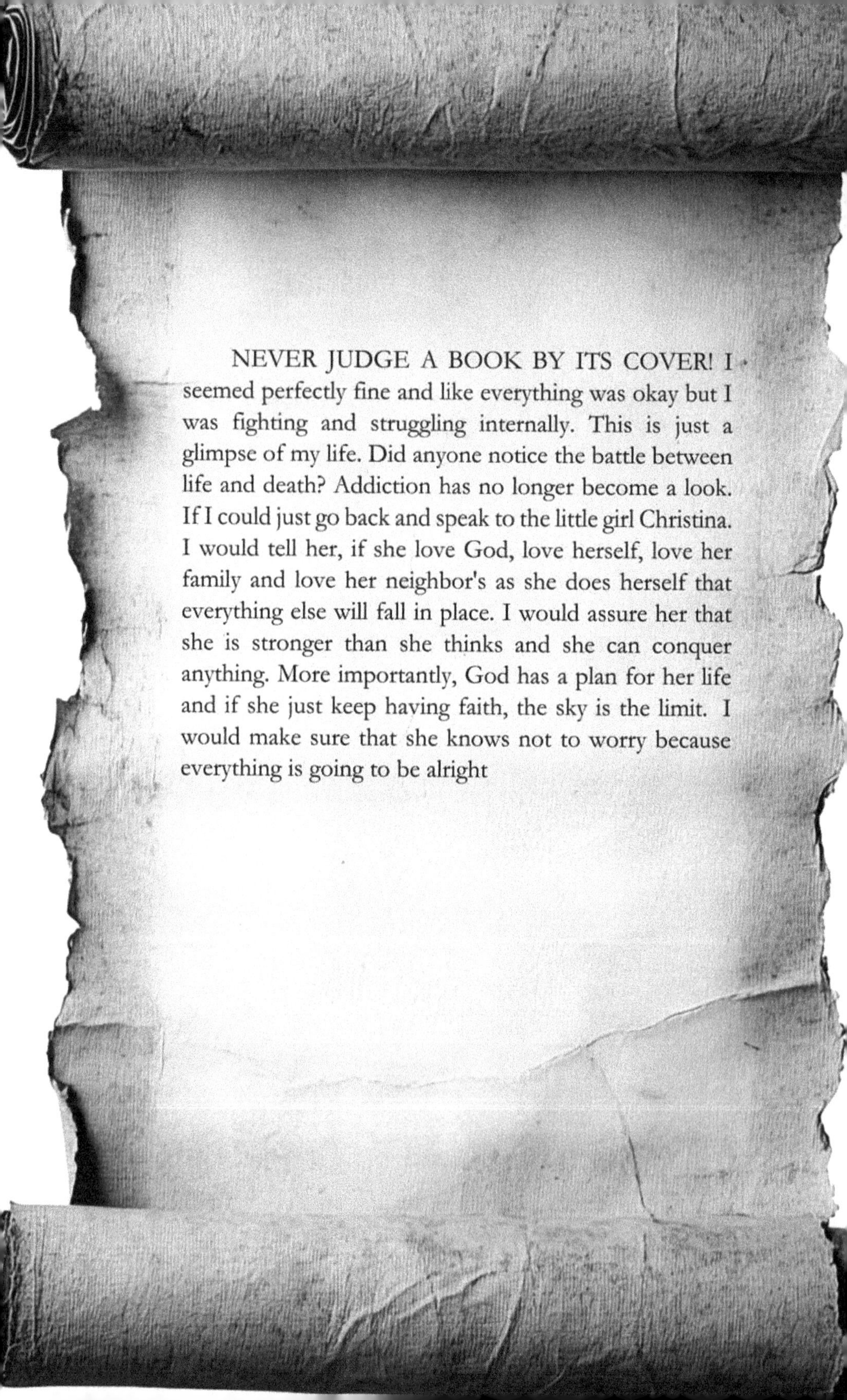

NEVER JUDGE A BOOK BY ITS COVER! I seemed perfectly fine and like everything was okay but I was fighting and struggling internally. This is just a glimpse of my life. Did anyone notice the battle between life and death? Addiction has no longer become a look. If I could just go back and speak to the little girl Christina. I would tell her, if she love God, love herself, love her family and love her neighbor's as she does herself that everything else will fall in place. I would assure her that she is stronger than she thinks and she can conquer anything. More importantly, God has a plan for her life and if she just keep having faith, the sky is the limit. I would make sure that she knows not to worry because everything is going to be alright

GALLERY

5th Sunday is Men's Day at Greater Miracle Temple. Today Deacon Donnell White shared his testimony of rekindling a healthy relationship with his daughter.
Each of them have experienced some tragic events in their lives, BUT God changes all things!

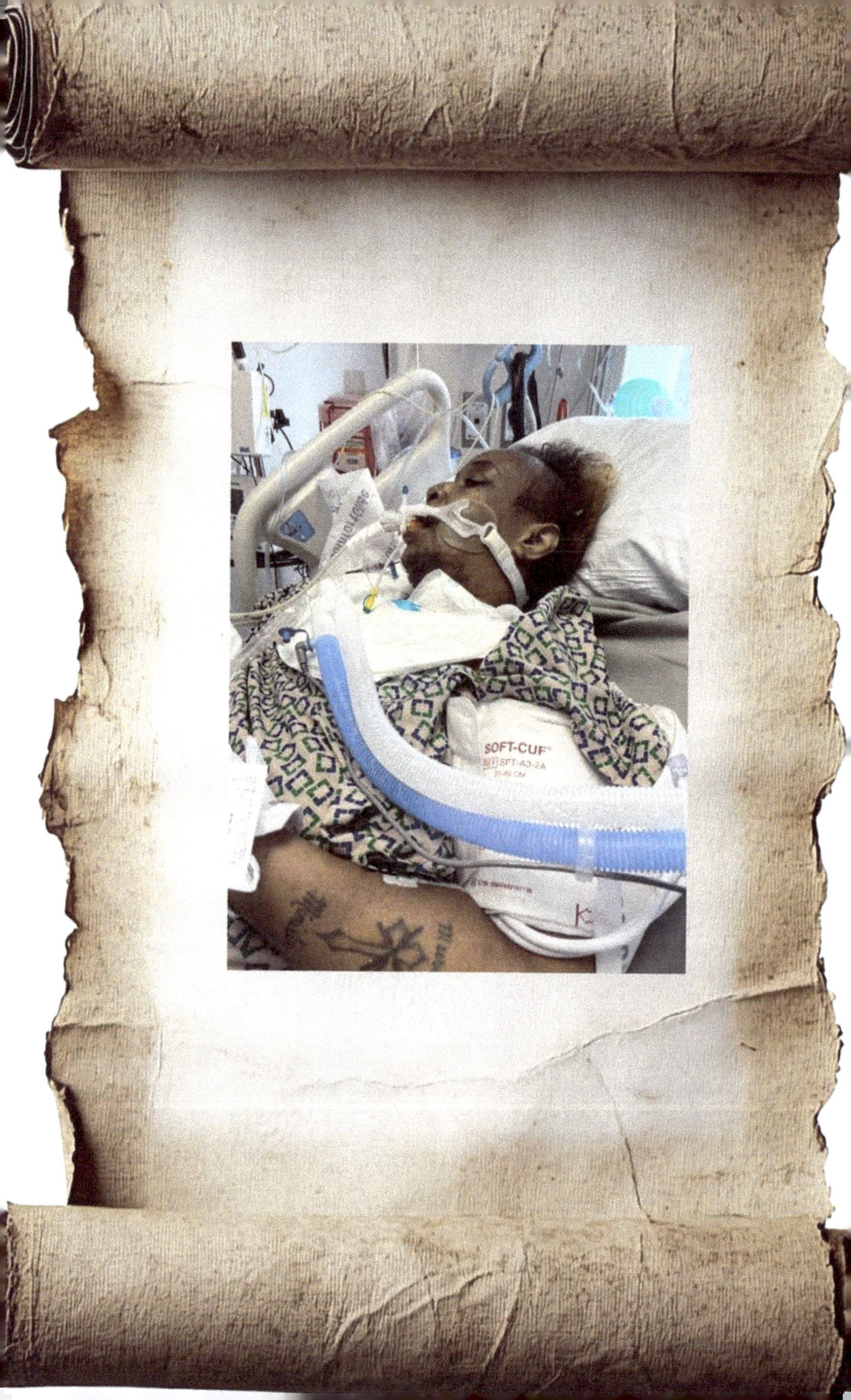

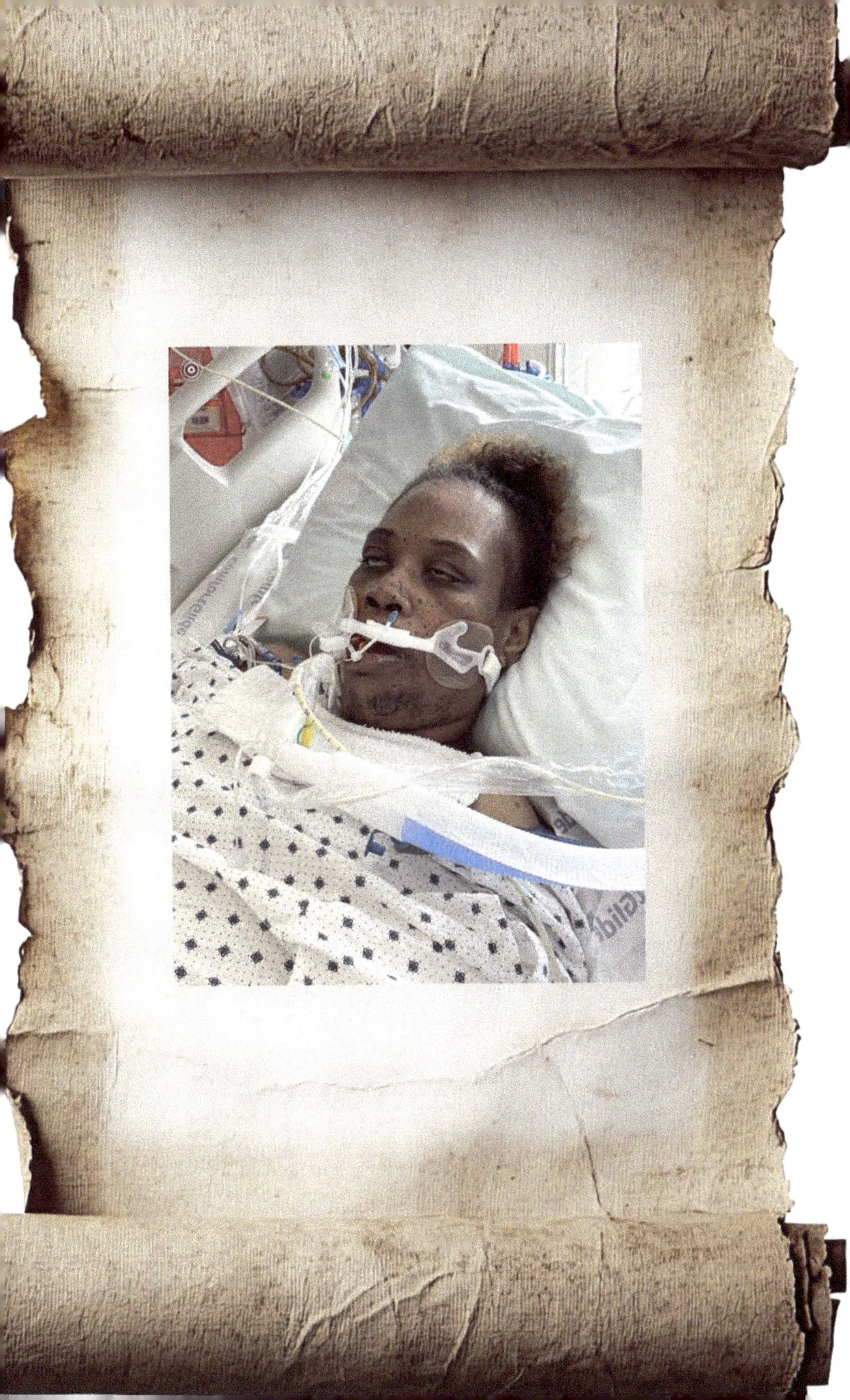

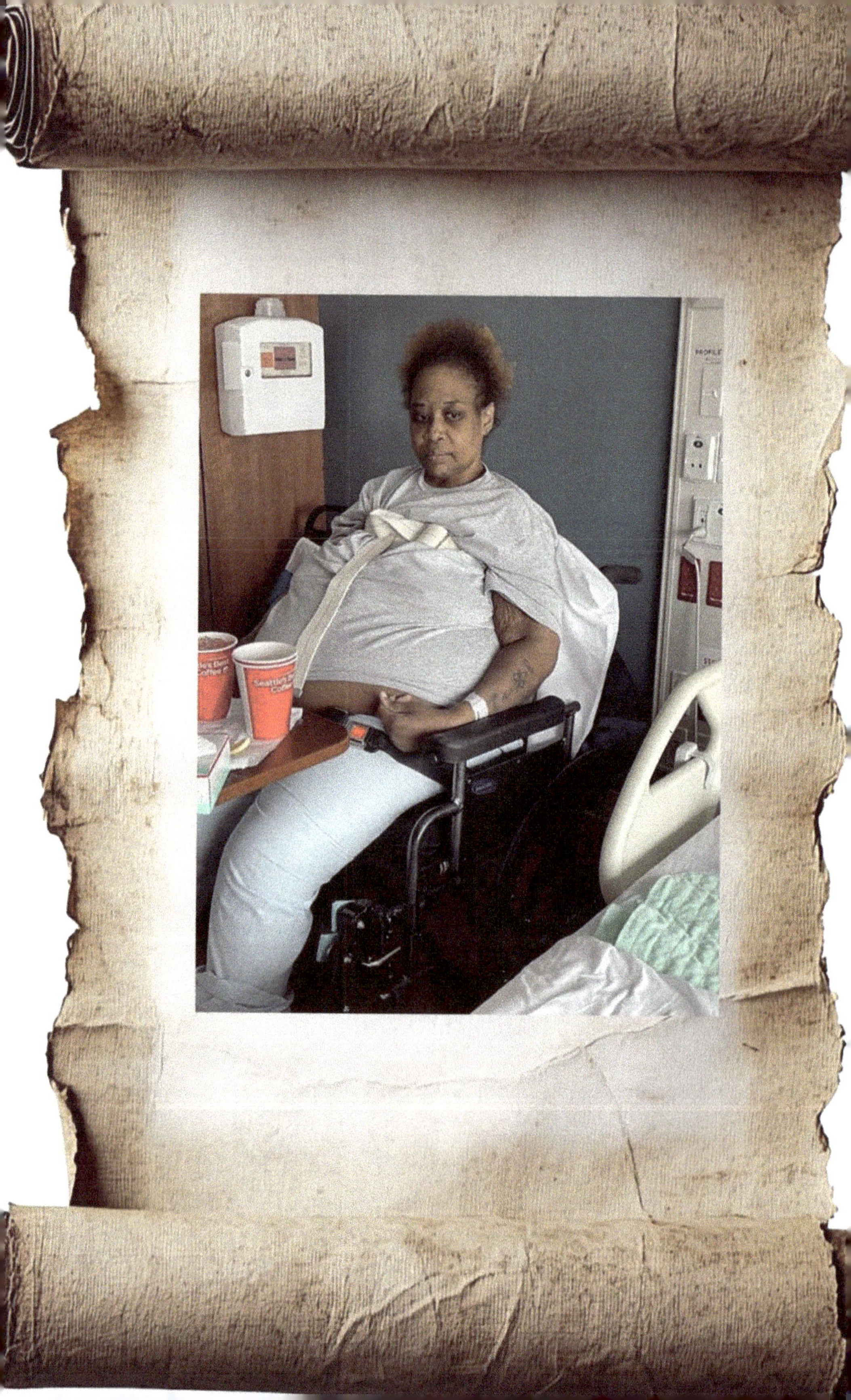

What emotions did this chapter evoke in you, and why do you think that is?

How does Christina Cloud's relationship with alcohol evolve in this chapter? What turning points or realizations stood out?

What coping mechanisms or patterns did the author describe that you found familiar or surprising?

____

____

____

____

____

____

____

____

____

____

____

____

____

____

How does the author use language or imagery to convey her internal struggles? Can you identify a passage that was particularly powerful?

What role do relationships (family, friends, partners) play in the author's journey in this chapter?

What societal or cultural messages about alcohol are challenged or reinforced in this chapter?

____

____

____

____

____

____

____

____

____

____

____

____

____

____

____

____

How does this chapter contribute to the overall narrative of healing and self-discovery?

____

____

____

____

____

____

____

____

____

____

____

____

____

____

What questions did this chapter leave you with about your own beliefs or experiences with addiction, recovery, or self-worth?